This

BOOK

BELONGS TO

_____

_____

DEDICATION

This Birding Journal Log book is dedicated to all the bird lovers out there who love bird watching and want to document their findings in the process.

You are my inspiration for producing books and I'm honored to be a part of keeping all of your Birdwatching notes and records organized.

This journal notebook will help you record your details about birdwatching.

Thoughtfully put together with these sections to record:

Season, Date, Location & Time, Weather & Elements, Place & Habitat, Sightings, Sounds & Activity, Bird Species, Markings, and Features, and Notes.

HOW TO USE THIS BOOK

The purpose of this book is to keep all of your Birding notes all in one place. It will help keep you organized.

This Birding Journal will allow you to accurately document every detail about your birdwatching adventures. It's a great way to chart your course through birding.

Here are examples of the prompts for you to fill in and write about your experience in this book:

1. **Season** - Write the season.

2. **Date & Time** - Log the date, day, and time.

3. **Location** - Record where you are birdwatching.

4. **Weather & Elements** - For recording what the weather and elements are like.

5. **Place & Habitat** - Write where you find them and all about their habitat in the field.

6. **Sightings** - Log everything about your bird sighting.

7. **Sounds & Activity** - Record all the sounds you hear and the activity & actions of the birds.

8. **Bird Species, Markings & Features** - Document the name species you have seen and any special markings or features.

9. **Notes** - Log any other important information ane details you will like. Also, a small space to draw pictures.

SEASON:
DATE: **TIME:**
LOCATION:

WEATHER/ELEMENTS

PLACE/LOCATION/HABITAT

SIGHTS/SOUNDS & ACTIVITY

BIRD SPECIES/MARKINGS/FEATURES

NOTES

SEASON:

DATE: **TIME:**

LOCATION:

WEATHER/ELEMENTS

PLACE/LOCATION/HABITAT

SIGHTS/SOUNDS & ACTIVITY

BIRD SPECIES/MARKINGS/FEATURES

NOTES

SEASON:
DATE: **TIME:**
LOCATION:

WEATHER/ELEMENTS

PLACE/LOCATION/HABITAT

SIGHTS/SOUNDS & ACTIVITY

BIRD SPECIES/MARKINGS/FEATURES

NOTES

SEASON:
DATE: **TIME:**
LOCATION:

WEATHER/ELEMENTS

PLACE/LOCATION/HABITAT

SIGHTS/SOUNDS & ACTIVITY

BIRD SPECIES/MARKINGS/FEATURES

NOTES

SEASON:

DATE: **TIME:**

LOCATION:

WEATHER/ELEMENTS

PLACE/LOCATION/HABITAT

SIGHTS/SOUNDS & ACTIVITY

BIRD SPECIES/MARKINGS/FEATURES

NOTES

SEASON:
DATE: **TIME:**
LOCATION:

WEATHER/ELEMENTS

PLACE/LOCATION/HABITAT

SIGHTS/SOUNDS & ACTIVITY

BIRD SPECIES/MARKINGS/FEATURES

NOTES

SEASON:
DATE: **TIME:**
LOCATION:

WEATHER/ELEMENTS

PLACE/LOCATION/HABITAT

SIGHTS/SOUNDS & ACTIVITY

BIRD SPECIES/MARKINGS/FEATURES

NOTES

SEASON:
DATE: **TIME:**
LOCATION:

WEATHER/ELEMENTS

PLACE/LOCATION/HABITAT

SIGHTS/SOUNDS & ACTIVITY

BIRD SPECIES/MARKINGS/FEATURES

NOTES

SEASON:

DATE: **TIME:**

LOCATION:

WEATHER/ELEMENTS

PLACE/LOCATION/HABITAT

SIGHTS/SOUNDS & ACTIVITY

BIRD SPECIES/MARKINGS/FEATURES

NOTES

SEASON:
DATE: **TIME:**
LOCATION:

WEATHER/ELEMENTS
PLACE/LOCATION/HABITAT

SIGHTS/SOUNDS & ACTIVITY

BIRD SPECIES/MARKINGS/FEATURES

NOTES

SEASON:

DATE: **TIME:**

LOCATION:

WEATHER/ELEMENTS

PLACE/LOCATION/HABITAT

SIGHTS/SOUNDS & ACTIVITY

BIRD SPECIES/MARKINGS/FEATURES

NOTES

SEASON:
DATE: **TIME:**
LOCATION:

WEATHER/ELEMENTS

PLACE/LOCATION/HABITAT

SIGHTS/SOUNDS & ACTIVITY

BIRD SPECIES/MARKINGS/FEATURES

NOTES

SEASON:

DATE: **TIME:**

LOCATION:

WEATHER/ELEMENTS
PLACE/LOCATION/HABITAT

SIGHTS/SOUNDS & ACTIVITY

BIRD SPECIES/MARKINGS/FEATURES

NOTES

SEASON:

DATE: **TIME:**

LOCATION:

WEATHER/ELEMENTS

PLACE/LOCATION/HABITAT

SIGHTS/SOUNDS & ACTIVITY

BIRD SPECIES/MARKINGS/FEATURES

NOTES

SEASON:
DATE: **TIME:**
LOCATION:

WEATHER/ELEMENTS

PLACE/LOCATION/HABITAT

SIGHTS/SOUNDS & ACTIVITY

BIRD SPECIES/MARKINGS/FEATURES

NOTES

SEASON:
DATE: **TIME:**
LOCATION:

WEATHER/ELEMENTS

PLACE/LOCATION/HABITAT

SIGHTS/SOUNDS & ACTIVITY

BIRD SPECIES/MARKINGS/FEATURES

NOTES

SEASON:
DATE: **TIME:**
LOCATION:

WEATHER/ELEMENTS

PLACE/LOCATION/HABITAT

SIGHTS/SOUNDS & ACTIVITY

BIRD SPECIES/MARKINGS/FEATURES

NOTES

SEASON:

DATE: **TIME:**

LOCATION:

WEATHER/ELEMENTS

PLACE/LOCATION/HABITAT

SIGHTS/SOUNDS & ACTIVITY

BIRD SPECIES/MARKINGS/FEATURES

NOTES

SEASON:
DATE: **TIME:**
LOCATION:

WEATHER/ELEMENTS

PLACE/LOCATION/HABITAT

SIGHTS/SOUNDS & ACTIVITY

BIRD SPECIES/MARKINGS/FEATURES

NOTES

SEASON:
DATE: **TIME:**
LOCATION:

WEATHER/ELEMENTS

PLACE/LOCATION/HABITAT

SIGHTS/SOUNDS & ACTIVITY

BIRD SPECIES/MARKINGS/FEATURES

NOTES

SEASON:
DATE: **TIME:**
LOCATION:

WEATHER/ELEMENTS

PLACE/LOCATION/HABITAT

SIGHTS/SOUNDS & ACTIVITY

BIRD SPECIES/MARKINGS/FEATURES

NOTES

SEASON:

DATE: **TIME:**

LOCATION:

WEATHER/ELEMENTS

PLACE/LOCATION/HABITAT

SIGHTS/SOUNDS & ACTIVITY

BIRD SPECIES/MARKINGS/FEATURES

NOTES

SEASON:
DATE: **TIME:**
LOCATION:

WEATHER/ELEMENTS
PLACE/LOCATION/HABITAT

SIGHTS/SOUNDS & ACTIVITY

BIRD SPECIES/MARKINGS/FEATURES

NOTES

SEASON:

DATE: **TIME:**

LOCATION:

WEATHER/ELEMENTS

PLACE/LOCATION/HABITAT

SIGHTS/SOUNDS & ACTIVITY

BIRD SPECIES/MARKINGS/FEATURES

NOTES

SEASON:
DATE: **TIME:**
LOCATION:

WEATHER/ELEMENTS

PLACE/LOCATION/HABITAT

SIGHTS/SOUNDS & ACTIVITY

BIRD SPECIES/MARKINGS/FEATURES

NOTES

SEASON:

DATE: **TIME:**

LOCATION:

WEATHER/ELEMENTS

PLACE/LOCATION/HABITAT

SIGHTS/SOUNDS & ACTIVITY

BIRD SPECIES/MARKINGS/FEATURES

NOTES

SEASON:

DATE: **TIME:**

LOCATION:

WEATHER/ELEMENTS

PLACE/LOCATION/HABITAT

SIGHTS/SOUNDS & ACTIVITY

BIRD SPECIES/MARKINGS/FEATURES

NOTES

SEASON:
DATE: **TIME:**
LOCATION:

WEATHER/ELEMENTS

PLACE/LOCATION/HABITAT

SIGHTS/SOUNDS & ACTIVITY

BIRD SPECIES/MARKINGS/FEATURES

NOTES

SEASON:
DATE: **TIME:**
LOCATION:

WEATHER/ELEMENTS

PLACE/LOCATION/HABITAT

SIGHTS/SOUNDS & ACTIVITY

BIRD SPECIES/MARKINGS/FEATURES

NOTES

SEASON:
DATE: **TIME:**
LOCATION:

WEATHER/ELEMENTS

PLACE/LOCATION/HABITAT

SIGHTS/SOUNDS & ACTIVITY

BIRD SPECIES/MARKINGS/FEATURES

NOTES

SEASON:
DATE: **TIME:**
LOCATION:

WEATHER/ELEMENTS

PLACE/LOCATION/HABITAT

SIGHTS/SOUNDS & ACTIVITY

BIRD SPECIES/MARKINGS/FEATURES

NOTES

SEASON:
DATE: **TIME:**
LOCATION:

WEATHER/ELEMENTS

PLACE/LOCATION/HABITAT

SIGHTS/SOUNDS & ACTIVITY

BIRD SPECIES/MARKINGS/FEATURES

NOTES

SEASON:
DATE: **TIME:**
LOCATION:

WEATHER/ELEMENTS

PLACE/LOCATION/HABITAT

SIGHTS/SOUNDS & ACTIVITY

BIRD SPECIES/MARKINGS/FEATURES

NOTES

SEASON:
DATE: **TIME:**
LOCATION:

WEATHER/ELEMENTS

PLACE/LOCATION/HABITAT

SIGHTS/SOUNDS & ACTIVITY

BIRD SPECIES/MARKINGS/FEATURES

NOTES

SEASON:
DATE: **TIME:**
LOCATION:

WEATHER/ELEMENTS

PLACE/LOCATION/HABITAT

SIGHTS/SOUNDS & ACTIVITY

BIRD SPECIES/MARKINGS/FEATURES

NOTES

SEASON:

DATE: **TIME:**

LOCATION:

WEATHER/ELEMENTS

PLACE/LOCATION/HABITAT

SIGHTS/SOUNDS & ACTIVITY

BIRD SPECIES/MARKINGS/FEATURES

NOTES

SEASON:

DATE: **TIME:**

LOCATION:

WEATHER/ELEMENTS

PLACE/LOCATION/HABITAT

SIGHTS/SOUNDS & ACTIVITY

BIRD SPECIES/MARKINGS/FEATURES

NOTES

SEASON:

DATE: **TIME:**

LOCATION:

WEATHER/ELEMENTS

PLACE/LOCATION/HABITAT

SIGHTS/SOUNDS & ACTIVITY

BIRD SPECIES/MARKINGS/FEATURES

NOTES

SEASON:
DATE: **TIME:**
LOCATION:

WEATHER/ELEMENTS

PLACE/LOCATION/HABITAT

SIGHTS/SOUNDS & ACTIVITY

BIRD SPECIES/MARKINGS/FEATURES

NOTES

SEASON:
DATE: **TIME:**
LOCATION:

WEATHER/ELEMENTS

PLACE/LOCATION/HABITAT

SIGHTS/SOUNDS & ACTIVITY

BIRD SPECIES/MARKINGS/FEATURES

NOTES

SEASON:
DATE: **TIME:**
LOCATION:

WEATHER/ELEMENTS

PLACE/LOCATION/HABITAT

SIGHTS/SOUNDS & ACTIVITY

BIRD SPECIES/MARKINGS/FEATURES

NOTES

SEASON:
DATE: **TIME:**
LOCATION:

WEATHER/ELEMENTS
PLACE/LOCATION/HABITAT

SIGHTS/SOUNDS & ACTIVITY

BIRD SPECIES/MARKINGS/FEATURES

NOTES

SEASON:

DATE: **TIME:**

LOCATION:

WEATHER/ELEMENTS

PLACE/LOCATION/HABITAT

SIGHTS/SOUNDS & ACTIVITY

BIRD SPECIES/MARKINGS/FEATURES

NOTES

SEASON:

DATE: **TIME:**

LOCATION:

WEATHER/ELEMENTS

PLACE/LOCATION/HABITAT

SIGHTS/SOUNDS & ACTIVITY

BIRD SPECIES/MARKINGS/FEATURES

NOTES

SEASON:
DATE: **TIME:**
LOCATION:

WEATHER/ELEMENTS

PLACE/LOCATION/HABITAT

SIGHTS/SOUNDS & ACTIVITY

BIRD SPECIES/MARKINGS/FEATURES

NOTES

SEASON:

DATE:　　　　　　　　　**TIME:**

LOCATION:

WEATHER/ELEMENTS

PLACE/LOCATION/HABITAT

SIGHTS/SOUNDS & ACTIVITY

BIRD SPECIES/MARKINGS/FEATURES

NOTES

SEASON:

DATE: **TIME:**

LOCATION:

WEATHER/ELEMENTS

PLACE/LOCATION/HABITAT

SIGHTS/SOUNDS & ACTIVITY

BIRD SPECIES/MARKINGS/FEATURES

NOTES

SEASON:
DATE: **TIME:**
LOCATION:

WEATHER/ELEMENTS
PLACE/LOCATION/HABITAT

SIGHTS/SOUNDS & ACTIVITY

BIRD SPECIES/MARKINGS/FEATURES

NOTES

SEASON:

DATE: **TIME:**

LOCATION:

WEATHER/ELEMENTS

PLACE/LOCATION/HABITAT

SIGHTS/SOUNDS & ACTIVITY

BIRD SPECIES/MARKINGS/FEATURES

NOTES

SEASON:
DATE: **TIME:**
LOCATION:

WEATHER/ELEMENTS
PLACE/LOCATION/HABITAT

SIGHTS/SOUNDS & ACTIVITY

BIRD SPECIES/MARKINGS/FEATURES

NOTES

SEASON:

DATE: **TIME:**

LOCATION:

WEATHER/ELEMENTS

PLACE/LOCATION/HABITAT

SIGHTS/SOUNDS & ACTIVITY

BIRD SPECIES/MARKINGS/FEATURES

NOTES

SEASON:
DATE: **TIME:**
LOCATION:

WEATHER/ELEMENTS

PLACE/LOCATION/HABITAT

SIGHTS/SOUNDS & ACTIVITY

BIRD SPECIES/MARKINGS/FEATURES

NOTES

SEASON:
DATE: **TIME:**
LOCATION:

WEATHER/ELEMENTS

PLACE/LOCATION/HABITAT

SIGHTS/SOUNDS & ACTIVITY

BIRD SPECIES/MARKINGS/FEATURES

NOTES

SEASON:
DATE: **TIME:**
LOCATION:

WEATHER/ELEMENTS

PLACE/LOCATION/HABITAT

SIGHTS/SOUNDS & ACTIVITY

BIRD SPECIES/MARKINGS/FEATURES

NOTES

SEASON:
DATE: **TIME:**
LOCATION:

WEATHER/ELEMENTS

PLACE/LOCATION/HABITAT

SIGHTS/SOUNDS & ACTIVITY

BIRD SPECIES/MARKINGS/FEATURES

NOTES

SEASON:
DATE: **TIME:**
LOCATION:

WEATHER/ELEMENTS

PLACE/LOCATION/HABITAT

SIGHTS/SOUNDS & ACTIVITY

BIRD SPECIES/MARKINGS/FEATURES

NOTES

SEASON:

DATE: **TIME:**

LOCATION:

WEATHER/ELEMENTS

PLACE/LOCATION/HABITAT

SIGHTS/SOUNDS & ACTIVITY

BIRD SPECIES/MARKINGS/FEATURES

NOTES

SEASON:

DATE: **TIME:**

LOCATION:

WEATHER/ELEMENTS
PLACE/LOCATION/HABITAT

SIGHTS/SOUNDS & ACTIVITY

BIRD SPECIES/MARKINGS/FEATURES

NOTES

SEASON:

DATE: **TIME:**

LOCATION:

WEATHER/ELEMENTS

PLACE/LOCATION/HABITAT

SIGHTS/SOUNDS & ACTIVITY

BIRD SPECIES/MARKINGS/FEATURES

NOTES

SEASON:
DATE: **TIME:**
LOCATION:

WEATHER/ELEMENTS

PLACE/LOCATION/HABITAT

SIGHTS/SOUNDS & ACTIVITY

BIRD SPECIES/MARKINGS/FEATURES

NOTES

SEASON:

DATE: **TIME:**

LOCATION:

WEATHER/ELEMENTS

PLACE/LOCATION/HABITAT

SIGHTS/SOUNDS & ACTIVITY

BIRD SPECIES/MARKINGS/FEATURES

NOTES

SEASON:

DATE: **TIME:**

LOCATION:

WEATHER/ELEMENTS

PLACE/LOCATION/HABITAT

SIGHTS/SOUNDS & ACTIVITY

BIRD SPECIES/MARKINGS/FEATURES

NOTES

SEASON:
DATE: **TIME:**
LOCATION:

WEATHER/ELEMENTS

PLACE/LOCATION/HABITAT

SIGHTS/SOUNDS & ACTIVITY

BIRD SPECIES/MARKINGS/FEATURES

NOTES

SEASON:

DATE: **TIME:**

LOCATION:

WEATHER/ELEMENTS

PLACE/LOCATION/HABITAT

SIGHTS/SOUNDS & ACTIVITY

BIRD SPECIES/MARKINGS/FEATURES

NOTES

SEASON:

DATE: **TIME:**

LOCATION:

WEATHER/ELEMENTS

PLACE/LOCATION/HABITAT

SIGHTS/SOUNDS & ACTIVITY

BIRD SPECIES/MARKINGS/FEATURES

NOTES

SEASON:

DATE: **TIME:**

LOCATION:

WEATHER/ELEMENTS

PLACE/LOCATION/HABITAT

SIGHTS/SOUNDS & ACTIVITY

BIRD SPECIES/MARKINGS/FEATURES

NOTES

SEASON:
DATE: **TIME:**
LOCATION:

WEATHER/ELEMENTS

PLACE/LOCATION/HABITAT

SIGHTS/SOUNDS & ACTIVITY

BIRD SPECIES/MARKINGS/FEATURES

NOTES

SEASON:
DATE: **TIME:**
LOCATION:

WEATHER/ELEMENTS
PLACE/LOCATION/HABITAT

SIGHTS/SOUNDS & ACTIVITY

BIRD SPECIES/MARKINGS/FEATURES

NOTES

SEASON:
DATE: **TIME:**
LOCATION:

WEATHER/ELEMENTS

PLACE/LOCATION/HABITAT

SIGHTS/SOUNDS & ACTIVITY

BIRD SPECIES/MARKINGS/FEATURES

NOTES

SEASON:

DATE: **TIME:**

LOCATION:

WEATHER/ELEMENTS

PLACE/LOCATION/HABITAT

SIGHTS/SOUNDS & ACTIVITY

BIRD SPECIES/MARKINGS/FEATURES

NOTES

SEASON:
DATE: **TIME:**
LOCATION:

WEATHER/ELEMENTS

PLACE/LOCATION/HABITAT

SIGHTS/SOUNDS & ACTIVITY

BIRD SPECIES/MARKINGS/FEATURES

NOTES

SEASON:
DATE: **TIME:**
LOCATION:

WEATHER/ELEMENTS

PLACE/LOCATION/HABITAT

SIGHTS/SOUNDS & ACTIVITY

BIRD SPECIES/MARKINGS/FEATURES

NOTES

SEASON:
DATE: **TIME:**
LOCATION:

WEATHER/ELEMENTS

PLACE/LOCATION/HABITAT

SIGHTS/SOUNDS & ACTIVITY

BIRD SPECIES/MARKINGS/FEATURES

NOTES

SEASON:

DATE: **TIME:**

LOCATION:

WEATHER/ELEMENTS

PLACE/LOCATION/HABITAT

SIGHTS/SOUNDS & ACTIVITY

BIRD SPECIES/MARKINGS/FEATURES

NOTES

SEASON:

DATE: **TIME:**

LOCATION:

WEATHER/ELEMENTS

PLACE/LOCATION/HABITAT

SIGHTS/SOUNDS & ACTIVITY

BIRD SPECIES/MARKINGS/FEATURES

NOTES

SEASON:
DATE: **TIME:**
LOCATION:

WEATHER/ELEMENTS

PLACE/LOCATION/HABITAT

SIGHTS/SOUNDS & ACTIVITY

BIRD SPECIES/MARKINGS/FEATURES

NOTES

SEASON:
DATE: **TIME:**
LOCATION:

WEATHER/ELEMENTS

PLACE/LOCATION/HABITAT

SIGHTS/SOUNDS & ACTIVITY

BIRD SPECIES/MARKINGS/FEATURES

NOTES

SEASON:
DATE: **TIME:**
LOCATION:

WEATHER/ELEMENTS
PLACE/LOCATION/HABITAT

SIGHTS/SOUNDS & ACTIVITY

BIRD SPECIES/MARKINGS/FEATURES

NOTES

SEASON:
DATE: **TIME:**
LOCATION:

WEATHER/ELEMENTS

PLACE/LOCATION/HABITAT

SIGHTS/SOUNDS & ACTIVITY

BIRD SPECIES/MARKINGS/FEATURES

NOTES

SEASON:

DATE: **TIME:**

LOCATION:

WEATHER/ELEMENTS

PLACE/LOCATION/HABITAT

SIGHTS/SOUNDS & ACTIVITY

BIRD SPECIES/MARKINGS/FEATURES

NOTES

SEASON:
DATE: **TIME:**
LOCATION:

WEATHER/ELEMENTS

PLACE/LOCATION/HABITAT

SIGHTS/SOUNDS & ACTIVITY

BIRD SPECIES/MARKINGS/FEATURES

NOTES

SEASON:
DATE: **TIME:**
LOCATION:

WEATHER/ELEMENTS
PLACE/LOCATION/HABITAT

SIGHTS/SOUNDS & ACTIVITY

BIRD SPECIES/MARKINGS/FEATURES

NOTES

SEASON:
DATE: **TIME:**
LOCATION:

WEATHER/ELEMENTS

PLACE/LOCATION/HABITAT

SIGHTS/SOUNDS & ACTIVITY

BIRD SPECIES/MARKINGS/FEATURES

NOTES

SEASON:

DATE: **TIME:**

LOCATION:

WEATHER/ELEMENTS
PLACE/LOCATION/HABITAT

SIGHTS/SOUNDS & ACTIVITY

BIRD SPECIES/MARKINGS/FEATURES

NOTES

SEASON:
DATE: **TIME:**
LOCATION:

WEATHER/ELEMENTS

PLACE/LOCATION/HABITAT

SIGHTS/SOUNDS & ACTIVITY

BIRD SPECIES/MARKINGS/FEATURES

NOTES

SEASON:

DATE: **TIME:**

LOCATION:

WEATHER/ELEMENTS

PLACE/LOCATION/HABITAT

SIGHTS/SOUNDS & ACTIVITY

BIRD SPECIES/MARKINGS/FEATURES

NOTES

SEASON:

DATE: **TIME:**

LOCATION:

WEATHER/ELEMENTS

PLACE/LOCATION/HABITAT

SIGHTS/SOUNDS & ACTIVITY

BIRD SPECIES/MARKINGS/FEATURES

NOTES

SEASON:
DATE: **TIME:**
LOCATION:

WEATHER/ELEMENTS

PLACE/LOCATION/HABITAT

SIGHTS/SOUNDS & ACTIVITY

BIRD SPECIES/MARKINGS/FEATURES

NOTES

SEASON:

DATE: **TIME:**

LOCATION:

WEATHER/ELEMENTS
PLACE/LOCATION/HABITAT

SIGHTS/SOUNDS & ACTIVITY

BIRD SPECIES/MARKINGS/FEATURES

NOTES

SEASON:

DATE: **TIME:**

LOCATION:

WEATHER/ELEMENTS

PLACE/LOCATION/HABITAT

SIGHTS/SOUNDS & ACTIVITY

BIRD SPECIES/MARKINGS/FEATURES

NOTES

SEASON:
DATE: **TIME:**
LOCATION:

WEATHER/ELEMENTS

PLACE/LOCATION/HABITAT

SIGHTS/SOUNDS & ACTIVITY

BIRD SPECIES/MARKINGS/FEATURES

NOTES

SEASON:
DATE: **TIME:**
LOCATION:

WEATHER/ELEMENTS
PLACE/LOCATION/HABITAT

SIGHTS/SOUNDS & ACTIVITY

BIRD SPECIES/MARKINGS/FEATURES

NOTES

SEASON:

DATE:　　　　　　　　　　**TIME:**

LOCATION:

WEATHER/ELEMENTS

PLACE/LOCATION/HABITAT

SIGHTS/SOUNDS & ACTIVITY

BIRD SPECIES/MARKINGS/FEATURES

NOTES

SEASON:
DATE: **TIME:**
LOCATION:

WEATHER/ELEMENTS

PLACE/LOCATION/HABITAT

SIGHTS/SOUNDS & ACTIVITY

BIRD SPECIES/MARKINGS/FEATURES

NOTES

SEASON:

DATE: **TIME:**

LOCATION:

WEATHER/ELEMENTS

PLACE/LOCATION/HABITAT

SIGHTS/SOUNDS & ACTIVITY

BIRD SPECIES/MARKINGS/FEATURES

NOTES

SEASON:

DATE: **TIME:**

LOCATION:

WEATHER/ELEMENTS

PLACE/LOCATION/HABITAT

SIGHTS/SOUNDS & ACTIVITY

BIRD SPECIES/MARKINGS/FEATURES

NOTES

SEASON:
DATE: **TIME:**
LOCATION:

WEATHER/ELEMENTS

PLACE/LOCATION/HABITAT

SIGHTS/SOUNDS & ACTIVITY

BIRD SPECIES/MARKINGS/FEATURES

NOTES

SEASON:

DATE:　　　　　　　　　　**TIME:**

LOCATION:

WEATHER/ELEMENTS

PLACE/LOCATION/HABITAT

SIGHTS/SOUNDS & ACTIVITY

BIRD SPECIES/MARKINGS/FEATURES

NOTES

SEASON:

DATE: **TIME:**

LOCATION:

WEATHER/ELEMENTS

PLACE/LOCATION/HABITAT

SIGHTS/SOUNDS & ACTIVITY

BIRD SPECIES/MARKINGS/FEATURES

NOTES

SEASON:
DATE: **TIME:**
LOCATION:

WEATHER/ELEMENTS

PLACE/LOCATION/HABITAT

SIGHTS/SOUNDS & ACTIVITY

BIRD SPECIES/MARKINGS/FEATURES

NOTES